Copyright 2021 by Color me Vintage

JOYEUX NOËL.

Have Fun at Christmas

More Vintage coloring books inspired by authentic vintage images by COLOR ME VINTAGE:

CHRISTMAS
Fashion POSTCARDS
A Christmas coloring book for adults

Grayscale coloring books for adults

Color me Vintage

grayscale coloring books for adults

NOSTALGIC VINTAGE

Color me Vintage

Grayscale Coloring
Books For Adults

BATHING BEAUTIES
Vintage

Beach coloring book adult

Color me Vintage

Retro Christmas SANTA
Christmas coloring book for adults grayscale

Old fashioned christmas coloring book inspired by authentic Santa Christmas greeting cards
Color me Vintage

Retro Christmas Cards
Coloring book for adults grayscale

Vintage christmas greetings coloring book
Color me Vintage

Join us @ Facebook
Twitter
Pinterest

www.ingramcontent.com/pod-product-compliance
Lightning Source LLC
LaVergne TN
LVHW061952070526
838199LV00060B/4084